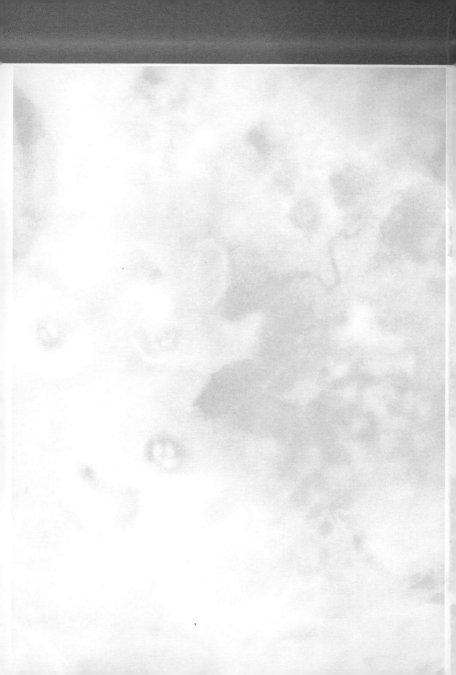

A

CELEBRATION
OF SIMPLICITY

Loving God & Enjoying Life

JOYCE MEYER

Harrison House

CONTENTS

THE
SIMPLICITY
OF FAITH

To enjoy life to the full, keep it simple.

GOD'S WORD FOR YOU

Now while they were on their way, it occurred that Jesus entered a certain village, and a woman named Martha received and welcomed Him into her house.

And she had a sister named Mary, who seated herself at the Lord's feet and was listening to His teaching.

But Martha [overly occupied and too busy] was distracted with much serving; and she came up to Him and said, Lord, is it nothing to You that my sister has left me to serve alone? Tell her then to help me [to lend a hand and do her part along with me]!

But the Lord replied to her by saying, Martha, Martha, you are anxious and troubled about many things; there is need of only one or but a few things. Mary has chosen the good portion [that which is to her advantage], which shall not be taken away from her.

LUKE 10:38-42

one

THE SIMPLICITY OF FAITH

believe that life should be a celebration. Far too many believers don't even enjoy life, let alone celebrate it. Many people truly love Jesus Christ and are on their way to heaven, but very few are enjoying the trip. For many years I was one of those people . . . and so was Martha.

Martha was busy doing what I used to do, running around trying to make everything perfect in order to impress God and everyone else. I complicated my relationship with the Lord because I had a legalistic approach to righteousness. I pursued many things— answers to my situations, prosperity, healing, success in my ministry, changes in my family. I only felt good about myself when I was accomplishing something. And I resented people like Mary, who enjoyed themselves. I thought they should be doing what I was doing.

My problem was that I was all Martha and no Mary. I loved Jesus, but I had not learned about the simple life He desired me to live. The answer, I discovered, was rooted in faith, discovering what it means to sit at the feet of Jesus, listen to His words, and trust God with all of my heart and soul.

If you want to live a complicated,
complex, joyless life, spend your time trying
to do something that can't be done without God.

GOD'S WORD FOR YOU

But I fear, lest somehow, as the serpent deceived Eve by his craftiness, so your minds may be corrupted from the simplicity that is in Christ.

2 CORINTHIANS 11:3 NKJV

In [this] freedom Christ has made us free [and completely liberated us]; stand fast then, and do not be hampered and held ensnared and submit again to a yoke of slavery [which you have once put off].

GALATIANS 5:1

ONLY JESUS!

Jesus came to this world and paid for our sins, taking our punishment upon Himself. He became our substitute, paid the debt we owed, at no cost to us. He did all this freely because of His great love, grace, and mercy. He inherited all the Father has to give and tells us that we are joint-heirs with Him by virtue of our faith. He has provided the way for our complete victory both here and hereafter. We are more than conquerors. He has conquered, and we get the reward without the battle.

How much simpler could it be? The gospel is wonderfully uncomplicated.

Complication is the work of Satan. He hates simplicity because he knows the power and the joy that our faith brings. Whenever your relationship with God becomes complex, bewildering, and confusing, consider the source—doubt and unbelief are being mixed and twisted together with belief.

Return to and celebrate the simplicity of your faith in Jesus alone!

*Believing is so much simpler
than not believing.*

GOD'S WORD FOR YOU

And He called a little child to Himself and put him in the midst of them and said, Truly I say to you, unless you repent (change, turn about) and become like little children [trusting, lowly, forgiving], you can never enter the kingdom of heaven [at all].

Whoever will humble himself therefore and become like this little child [trusting, lowly, loving, forgiving] is greatest in the kingdom of heaven.

MATTHEW 18:2-4

So if the Son liberates you [makes you free men], then you are really and unquestionably free.

JOHN 8:36

GLORIOUS FREEDOM

Children believe what they are told. Some people say children are gullible; meaning they believe anything no matter how ridiculous it sounds. But children are not gullible; they are trusting. It is a child's nature to trust unless he has experienced something that teaches him otherwise. And another thing we all know about children is that they can literally enjoy just about anything, even turning work into games.

Our heavenly Father desires us to come to Him as children. He wants us to know that we are His precious little ones and to put our complete faith in Him to care for us. He wants us to take His hand and lean on Him, continually asking for His help. Everything that God calls us to do, He must help us do. He is ready, waiting, and more than willing. But we must come humbly as little children—sincere, unpretentious, honest, open—knowing that without Him, we can do nothing.

As God's children we were never intended to live in bondage of any kind. We should be experiencing glorious freedom and liberty—freedom to enjoy all that God has given us in Christ. He has given us life, and our goal should be to enjoy it.

Seek to become and remain childlike with all the simplicity of a child. It will enhance the quality of your life in a most amazing way.

GOD'S WORD FOR YOU

Some trust in and boast of chariots and some of horses, but we will trust in and boast of the name of the Lord our God.

PSALM 20:7

Lean on, trust in, and be confident in the Lord with all your heart and mind and do not rely on your own insight or understanding.

PROVERBS 3:5

Marvelous Dividends

There are many facets of faith. The most brilliant facet, however, is trust! Trust is something we have, and we decide what to do with it. We decide in whom or in what to put our trust.

Where have you placed your trust? Is your trust in your job, employer, bank account, or friends? Perhaps your trust is in yourself, your past record of successes, education, natural talents, or possessions. All of these are temporal, subject to change. Only the Lord changes not. He alone is the Rock that cannot be moved.

As children of God, we must remember Who delivered us in the past and know Who will deliver us in current troubles, then take our trust and put it in the right place, which is in God alone. Trust is not upset, because it has entered into God's rest. Trust is not confused, because it has no need to lean to its own understanding. Trust does not indulge in carnal reasoning; it lets God be God.

❦

Choose to place your trust in God. It requires a greater faith, but it pays marvelous dividends.

GOD'S WORD FOR YOU

Jesus replied, This is the work (service) that God asks of you: that you believe.

JOHN 6:29

Truly I tell you, whoever says to this mountain, Be lifted up and thrown into the sea! and does not doubt at all in his heart but believes that what he says will take place, it will be done for him.

For this reason I am telling you, whatever you ask for in prayer, believe (trust and be confident) that it is granted to you, and you will [get it].

MARK 11:23-24

BELIEVE!

God's plan for us is actually so simple that many times we miss it. We tend to look for something more complicated—something more difficult—that we are expected to do to please God. Jesus has told us what we are to do to please the Father, "Believe!"

Doubt brings in confusion and often depression. It causes us to speak doubtful and negative words. Believing, on the other hand, releases joy and leaves us free to enjoy life while God is taking care of our circumstances. It sounds almost too good to be true, which is why many people never enter into God's plan.

When Jesus said that whatever we ask of God, believing, will be granted to us, He was saying that we will receive it *free*. In God's economy, everything comes to us as a gift, and the only thing we can do with a gift is receive it graciously with a thankful heart.

Faith is not the price that buys God's blessing. It is the hand that receives His blessing. The price was paid for us by Jesus Christ on the cross.

Faith, like muscle, is strengthened
by "using" it, not by talking about it.

GOD'S WORD FOR YOU

For it is by free grace (God's unmerited favor)
that you are saved (delivered from judgment and made
partakers of Christ's salvation) through [your] faith.
And this [salvation] is not of yourselves [of your own
doing, it came not through your own striving], but it is
the gift of God;

Not because of works [not the fulfillment of the Law's
demands], lest any man should boast. [It is not the result
of what anyone can possibly do, so no one can pride
himself in it or take glory to himself.]

EPHESIANS 2:8-9

For we have heard of your faith in Christ Jesus [the
leaning of your entire human personality on Him in
absolute trust and confidence in His power, wisdom, and
goodness] and of the love which you [have and show] for
all the saints (God's consecrated ones).

COLOSSIANS 1:4

FAITH AND GRACE

Over the past ten years I heard so much about faith that I was about to kill myself trying to believe God for all kinds of stuff without understanding the grace of God. I didn't know how to lean on God, how to rely on the Lord, how to totally trust my heavenly Father in every situation of life. The problem was that I was trusting my faith to meet my needs rather than trusting my God.

If everything is based on our faith alone, we will end up frustrated, trying to make things happen that we have no power to make happen. I was trying to believe God for healing and prosperity and a happy family life—and it wasn't working. So I tried to believe God more, which only led to more frustration, unhappiness, and discouragement.

The mistake I made was trying to make things happen by faith, by believing God. Instead, I had to learn to get beyond that to relying on the grace of God. When I did that, when I gave up all my works, then my frustration ceased. I realized that no matter how much faith I had, if God did not come through my faith by His grace to answer my needs, I was never going to receive anything.

The Holy Spirit works to get our eyes off our ability to believe and onto God's faithfulness and willingness to meet our need.

GOD'S WORD FOR YOU

. . . *be vigilant and cautious at all times; for that enemy of yours, the devil, roams around like a lion roaring [in fierce hunger], seeking someone to seize upon and devour.*

Withstand him; be firm in faith [against his onset— rooted, established, strong, immovable, and determined].

1 PETER 5:8-9

So be subject to God. Resist the devil [stand firm against him], and he will flee from you.

JAMES 4:7

THE PURPOSE OF FAITH

We must remember that the devil is not going to just sit back and allow us to take new ground without putting up a fight. Any time we begin to make progress in building the Kingdom of God, our enemy is going to come against us.

Many times the mistake we make is trying to use faith to get to the place where there is total freedom from trouble. The purpose of faith is not always to keep us from having trouble; it is often to carry us through trouble. If we never had any trouble, we wouldn't need any faith.

The temptation exists to run away from our problems, but the Lord says that we are to go through them. The good news is that He has promised that we will never have to go through them alone. He will always be there to help us in every way. He has said to us, "Fear not, for I am with you."

In our daily experience, we must learn to stand our ground and back the devil off our property, to drive him out of different areas of our lives. Learning to be stable in hard times is one of the best ways to do this.

The devil will give up when he sees that you are not going to give in.

GOD'S WORD FOR YOU

I have learned how to be content (satisfied to the point where I am not disturbed or disquieted) in whatever state I am.

PHILIPPIANS 4:11

FAITH AND CONTENTMENT

The Bible teaches us to be content no matter what our circumstances may be (Hebrews 13:5 KJV). We are not to be upset about anything, no matter what is happening. Instead, we are to pray about it and tell God our need. While we are waiting for Him to move, we are to be thankful for all that God has done for us already (Philippians 4:6).

I have discovered that the secret of being content is to ask God for what I want, knowing that if it is right, He will bring it to pass at the right time. And if it is not right, He will do something much better than what I asked for.

We must learn to trust God completely if we ever intend to enjoy peaceful living. We must meditate on what God has done in our life instead of what we are still waiting on Him to do.

God loves you. He is a good God Who only does good things. Be content knowing that His way is perfect, and He brings with Him a great recompense of reward for those who trust in Him (Hebrews 10:35 KJV).

Trust God. Hide yourself in Him.

God is working in secret, behind the scenes even when it looks as though nothing will ever change.

GOD'S WORD FOR YOU

Therefore humble yourselves . . . casting the whole of your care [all your anxieties, all your worries, all your concerns, once and for all] on Him, for He cares for you affectionately and cares about you watchfully.

1 PETER 5:6-7

HE CARES FOR YOU

Worry, anxiety, and care have no positive effect on our lives. They do not bring a solution to problems. They do not help us achieve good health, and they prevent our growth in the Word of God.

One of the ways that Satan steals the Word of God from our heart is through cares. The Bible says we are to cast our cares onto God, which is done by prayer. We cannot handle our own problems; we are not built for it. We are created by God to be dependent upon Him, to bring Him our challenges, and to allow Him to help us with them.

We must not take the care upon ourselves. Keeping our cares is a manifestation of pride. It shows that we think we can solve our own problems and that we don't need the Lord.

We show our humility by leaning on God. Worry, anxiety, and care are not manifestations of leaning on God, but they clearly state by their mere existence that we are attempting to take care of ourselves.

Pray about everything and worry about nothing. You will enjoy life much more.

God's ability to bring His will to pass in your life is determined by your faith in Him and in His Word.

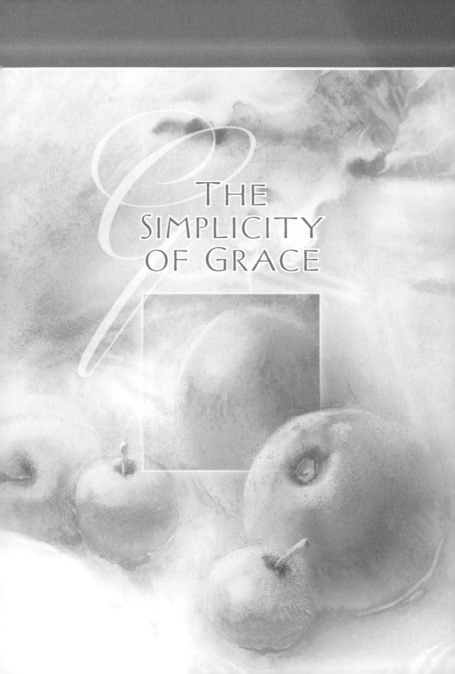

THE
SIMPLICITY
OF GRACE

Grace is God doing us a favor,
coming in with His power and might
to accomplish in and through us
what we don't deserve for Him to do.

GOD'S WORD FOR YOU

Let me ask you this one question: Did you receive the [Holy] Spirit as the result of obeying the Law and doing its works, or was it by hearing [the message of the Gospel] and believing [it]? [Was it from observing a law of rituals or from a message of faith?]

Are you so foolish and so senseless and so silly? Having begun [your new life spiritually] with the [Holy] Spirit, are you now reaching perfection [by dependence] on the flesh?

Have you suffered so many things and experienced so much all for nothing (to no purpose)—if it really is to no purpose and in vain?

Then does He Who supplies you with His marvelous [Holy] Spirit and works powerfully and miraculously among you do so on [the grounds of your doing] what the Law demands, or because of your believing in and adhering to and trusting in and relying on the message that you heard?

GALATIANS 3:2-5

two

THE SIMPLICITY
OF GRACE

There is nothing more powerful than the grace of God. Everything in the Bible—salvation, the infilling of the Holy Spirit, fellowship with God, and all victory in our daily lives—is based upon it. Without grace, we are nothing, we have nothing, can do nothing. If it were not for the grace of God, we would all be miserable and hopeless.

The grace of God is not complicated or confusing. In fact, it is so simple that many of us miss its true meaning and end up making our lives incredibly complex. I know I did.

Reading God's Word, I constantly saw the need for change in my life. But I didn't know that the grace of God could bring about those changes. I didn't know how to allow the Holy Spirit to come into my life and cause the things to happen. So I tried to change myself to be everything the Word said I was to be. I also tried to change everything else in my life—my husband, my children, and any circumstances I thought were the cause of my problems. The results went beyond frustration into becoming destructive.

I thank God that He did not leave me there.

Grace is the power of God available to meet our needs without any cost to us. It is received by believing rather than through our own effort.

GOD'S WORD FOR YOU

But He gives us more and more grace (power of the Holy Spirit, to meet this evil tendency and all others fully). . . . God sets Himself against the proud . . . but gives grace [continually] to the lowly (those who are humble enough to receive it).

JAMES 4:6

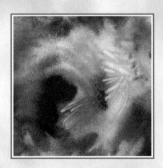

MORE AND MORE GRACE

All human beings have evil tendencies, but James teaches us that God will give us more and more grace to meet these tendencies.

I spent much of my Christian life trying to overcome my own wrong motives and intentions. All my trying brought much frustration. I had to come to a place of humility. I had to learn that God gives grace to the humble—not the proud.

We have our own ideas about what we can accomplish, but often we think more highly of ourselves than we ought. We should have a humble attitude, knowing that apart from God, we can do nothing.

If you are planning your own way, trying to make things happen in the strength of your own flesh, then you are frustrated. You probably have said, "No matter what I do, nothing seems to work!" Nothing will ever work until you learn to trust in God's grace.

Relax. Let God be God. Stop being so hard on yourself. Change is a process; it comes little by little. You're on your way to perfection, so enjoy the trip.

If you desire to be free, you must be willing to exchange trying for trusting. You must be willing to stop doing and start asking.

GOD'S WORD FOR YOU

But that no man is justified by the law in the sight of God, it is evident: for, The just shall live by faith.

And the law is not faith: but, The man that doeth them shall live in them.

Christ hath redeemed us from the curse of the law, being made a curse for us: for it is written, Cursed is every one that hangeth on a tree.

GALATIANS 3:11-13 KJV

[Therefore, I do not treat God's gracious gift as something of minor importance and defeat its very purpose]; I do not set aside and invalidate and frustrate and nullify the grace (unmerited favor) of God. For if justification (righteousness, acquittal from guilt) comes through [observing the ritual of] the Law, then Christ (the Messiah) died groundlessly and to no purpose and in vain. [His death was then wholly superfluous.]

GALATIANS 2:21

GRACE VERSUS WORKS

It is curious that we come to God through Christ just as we are, relying on nothing but the blood of Jesus to cleanse us from our sins. Our hearts are full of gratitude because we know we don't deserve it. But from that moment on, for some reason we want to deserve everything else He gives us. From then on, God has to practically force every single blessing upon us because we think we don't deserve it. We didn't read the Bible enough, didn't pray enough, or lost our temper in traffic. We find a million ways to be disqualified from God's favor.

Despite all our emphasis on faith, we try to live by works a life that was brought into being and designed by God to be lived by grace. It's no wonder we feel frustrated and confused—both are signs that we are out of grace and into works.

When you have a problem in your life that you do not know how to handle, what you need is not more figuring and reasoning, but more grace. If you can't find a solution to your problem, then you need the Lord to reveal it to you.

The more you fret and strain over it, the more unlikely you are to see the solution to it.

Where works fail, grace always succeeds.
Do not frustrate the grace of God.

GOD'S WORD FOR YOU

So I asked the angel who talked with me, What are these, my lord?

Then the angel who talked with me answered me, Do you not know what these are? And I said, No, my lord.

Then he said to me, This [addition of the bowl to the candlestick, causing it to yield a ceaseless supply of oil from the olive trees] is the word of the Lord to Zerubbabel, saying, Not by might, nor by power, but by My Spirit [of Whom the oil is a symbol], says the Lord of hosts.

ZECHARIAH 4:4-6

GET PLUGGED IN!

In our Christian walk, many times we end up with a lot of principles, formulas, and methods, but no real power. That may be true for teachings on faith, prayer, praise, meditation, Bible study, confession, spiritual warfare, and all the other precepts we have been hearing about and engaging in. They are all good, and we need to know about them, but alone they cannot solve our problems.

We must remember that, as good as all these disciplines are, they are only channels to receiving from the Lord. They are of no help unless they are plugged into the divine power source.

We get plugged in through a personal relationship with God, which requires time. We will never have any real lasting victory in our Christian life without spending time in personal, private fellowship with the Lord. He has an individual plan for you. If you ask Him, He will come into your heart and commune with you. He will teach and guide you in the way you should go.

Learn to respond quickly to the promptings of the Holy Spirit. Come apart with Him privately, and you will be rewarded in abundance.

*It is only in the presence of the Lord
that we receive the power of the Lord.*

GOD'S WORD FOR YOU

Now to a laborer, his wages are not counted as a favor or a gift, but as an obligation (something owed to him).

But to one who, not working [by the Law], trusts (believes fully) in Him Who justifies the ungodly, his faith is credited to him as righteousness (the standing acceptable to God).

ROMANS 4:4-5

Through Him also we have [our] access (entrance, introduction) by faith into this grace (state of God's favor) in which we [firmly and safely] stand. And let us rejoice and exult in our hope of experiencing and enjoying the glory of God.

ROMANS 5:2

GRACE IS NOT FOR SALE

The devil wants you and me to think that we can buy the grace of God. But God's grace is not for sale, because by its very definition—*unmerited* favor—it is a gift.

Grace cannot be bought by prayer, good works, Bible readings, or confessing Scriptures. It cannot even be bought by faith. The grace of God is receivable, but it is not "buyable."

We must be very careful that even when we operate by all the right methods our motives are pure. Even when we are fellowshipping with the Lord, if our motive is to get something from Him, we have moved from grace to works. Let us not fall into the trap of thinking that we *deserve* anything good from the Lord. Anytime we get wrapped up in self and ego we are on dangerous ground. We must get beyond ourselves and our works and efforts and keep our eyes focused on God and His grace toward us.

We are to seek the Lord and to fellowship with Him for no other reason than the fact that we love Him and want to be in His presence.

Determination and willpower can only take you so far. When the flesh fizzles out—and it will—the whole thing will collapse, and so will you.

GOD'S WORD FOR YOU

Now unto him that is able to do exceeding abundantly above all that we ask or think, according to the power that worketh in us, unto him be glory in the church by Christ Jesus throughout all ages, world without end. Amen.

EPHESIANS 3:20 KJV

But He said, What is impossible with men is possible with God.

LUKE 18:27

THE DIVINE ENABLER

Our God is able to do far above and beyond anything that we can ever dare to hope, ask, or even think. We need to pray, to do the asking, in faith, in trust. That opens the channel. But it is God Who does the work, not us.

If you are struggling with changes that need to be made in your own personality, this word is especially for you. You can't change yourself. But thanks be to God, He can! He knows what is wrong with you, and He's ready and able to bring about the changes that you need if you just ask.

You and I don't have a problem that is too big for the grace of God. If our problem gets bigger, God's grace gets bigger. If our problem multiplies, so that we go from one to two or three or more, the grace of God also multiplies so that we are able to handle them.

It doesn't take any more faith to believe God for the answer to three problems than for the answer to two problems or even one problem. Either we believe our God is big enough to handle whatever we face, or we do not.

We think we are supposed to be achievers, and we are. But the way we achieve is to believe. That frees us from worry and reasoning.

GOD'S WORD FOR YOU

Let us then fearlessly and confidently and boldly draw near to the throne of grace (the throne of God's unmerited favor to us sinners), that we may receive mercy [for our failures] and find grace to help in good time for every need [appropriate help and well-timed help, coming just when we need it].

HEBREWS 4:16

MOUNTAINS OF GRACE

Our God is always with us. But sometimes mountains rise in front of us that seem bigger than He is. The temptation is to avoid the obstacles, to run away from the things that oppose us. In reality, we are running from the enemy, because he is the one who throws up the obstacles for that very purpose. I encourage you to face the enemy, to not be afraid or intimidated by what he throws at you.

One of the aspects that we fail to understand about God's grace is that although He has endless mountains of it, we must come to His throne constantly for assurance about today, peace about yesterday, and confidence about tomorrow. Though God is always leading us into situations that are over our head, He knows exactly what He's going to do. He has a plan, a path, and a work all ready for us.

No matter what happens, God is still in control. His grace is power, and it is sufficient to meet all our needs. Even through the most difficult of times, times of extraordinary pressure and stress, His divine, wonder-working power is equal to all life's challengers. Call on the Lord and He will provide.

God never leads us where He cannot keep us.
His grace is always sufficient for us —
in any and every circumstance of life.

GOD'S WORD FOR YOU

God selected (deliberately chose) what in the world is foolish to put the wise to shame, and what the world calls weak to put the strong to shame.

And God also selected (deliberately chose) what in the world is low-born and insignificant and branded and treated with contempt, even the things that are nothing, that He might depose and bring to nothing the things that are.

So that no mortal man should [have pretense for glorying and] boast in the presence of God.

1 CORINTHIANS 1:27-29

GRACE TO BE HIS AMBASSADORS

One time while I was reading about Smith Wigglesworth and his great faith, I was deeply impressed by all the wonderful things he did in his ministry. I thought, *Lord, I know I'm called, but I could never do anything like that.* Just that quickly, I sensed the Lord speak to my heart, "Why not? Aren't you as big a mess as anybody else?"

You see, we have it backward. We think God is looking for people who "have it all together." But that is not true. The Word of God says that God in His grace and favor chooses the weak and foolish things of the world in order to confound the wise. He is looking for those who will humble themselves and allow Him to work His will through them.

If you will be careful not to get haughty or arrogant, the Lord can use you just as mightily as any of the other great men and women of God. He doesn't choose us because we are able, but simply because we are available. That too is part of God's grace and favor that He pours out upon us when He chooses us as Christ's personal ambassadors.

You have as much right to God's favor as anyone else. Learn to avail yourself of it and walk in it.

GOD'S WORD FOR YOU

And I will pour out upon the house of David and upon the inhabitants of Jerusalem the Spirit of grace or unmerited favor and supplication.

ZECHARIAH 12:10

Now the Lord is the Spirit, and where the Spirit of the Lord is, there is liberty (emancipation from bondage, freedom).

And all of us, as with unveiled face, [because we] continued to behold [in the Word of God] as in a mirror the glory of the Lord, are constantly being transfigured into His very own image in ever increasing splendor and from one degree of glory to another; [for this comes] from the Lord [Who is] the Spirit.

2 CORINTHIANS 3:17-18

THE SPIRIT OF GRACE

One of the twenty-five biblical names used to refer to the Holy Spirit is the Spirit of grace and supplication. There is no way to live in victory without understanding the Holy Spirit's role in empowering our lives and in teaching us to pray, asking God for what we need rather than trying to make it happen on our own.

The Spirit of grace is the One Who brings every good gift into our life, everything we need. His multiple role as Comforter, Counselor, Helper, Intercessor, Advocate, Strengthener, and Standby can be summarized by saying that His purpose is to get right in the middle of our lives and make them all work out for the glory of God.

God is interested in every detail of your life. He wants to help with everything in your life. He stands by us at all times waiting for the first available opportunity to jump in and give us the help and strength we need. Learn one of the most spiritual prayers you can offer: "Help!" We have not because we ask not. Ask and ask and ask. Keep on asking so that you may receive and your joy may be full.

The grace of God doesn't just fall upon us; we must choose it. God's part is to give us His grace and Spirit; our part is to give Him our mind and will.

THE
SIMPLICITY OF
JOY AND PEACE

This is God's will for us, that we might have and enjoy life. Jesus did not die for you and me that we might be miserable. He died to deliver us from every kind of oppression and misery.

GOD'S WORD FOR YOU

For the kingdom of God is not meat and drink; but righteousness, and peace, and joy in the Holy Ghost.

ROMANS 14:17 KJV

May the God of your hope so fill you with all joy and peace in believing [through the experience of your faith] that by the power of the Holy Spirit you may abound and be overflowing (bubbling over) with hope.

ROMANS 15:13

three

THE SIMPLICITY
OF JOY AND PEACE

t should never be this complicated, I thought, feeling miserable. Something was lurking inside, constantly draining the joy out of me. It began to dawn on me that I was doubting instead of believing. I was doubting the call of God on my life, wondering if He would meet our financial needs, questioning my decisions and actions.

I had become negative instead of positive. I was doubting instead of believing.

Doubt complicates everything. It creeps in through the door of your heart, filling your mind with reasoning that leads to negativity. It rotates around and around the circumstances or situations of your life, attempting to find answers for them.

The Word of God does not instruct us to search for our own answers. We are, however, instructed to trust God with all of our heart and soul (Proverbs 3:5). When we follow the simple guidelines the Lord has laid out for us, they will unerringly bring us to joy and peace.

When doubt knocks at your door, answer with a believing heart, and you'll always maintain the victory. That's a grand reason to celebrate.

*Joy is never released through unbelief
but is always present where there is belief.*

GOD'S WORD FOR YOU

*For the kingdom of God is not meat and drink; but
righteousness, and peace, and joy in the Holy Ghost.*

ROMANS 14:17 KJV

JOY

My understanding of *joy* is that it covers a wide range of emotions, from calm delight to extreme hilarity. The hilarious times are fun, and we all need those moments of laughing until our sides hurt. We probably won't live our daily lives that way, but we need those times. Why else would God give us the ability to laugh?

As Christians, we should grow in our ability to enjoy life and be able to say, "I live my life in a state of calm delight." I think calm delight is a mixture of peace and joy.

Some of the Greek words relating to joy in the Bible mean *delight, gladness, exceeding joyful, exuberant joy, to exult, rejoice greatly . . . with exceeding joy.* Webster defines it as *great pleasure or happiness, a source of pleasure or satisfaction, to fill with joy, or to enjoy.*

Whichever definition you prefer, the sad reality is that so few believers know the joy of the Lord. Don't let another day pass by without experiencing the Kingdom of God at its center—righteousness, peace, and joy in the Holy Spirit.

There is nothing as tragic
as being alive and not enjoying life.

GOD'S WORD FOR YOU

The thief comes only to steal and kill and destroy; I
have come that they may have life, and have it to the full.

JOHN 10:10 NIV

CELEBRATE LIFE

It is possible to live our lives blandly going through the motions of working, accomplishing, doing, but to never truly enjoy life. This is true of unbelievers, as well as believers, who have not learned to really enjoy the life God has given them. Jesus gave us life so we can derive pleasure from being alive, not just so we can go through the motions and try to survive until He comes back for us or takes us home.

Enjoying life is a decision that is not based on enjoyable circumstances. It is an attitude of the heart, a decision to enjoy everything because everything— even little, seemingly insignificant things—has a part in God's overall "big picture."

Doubt and unbelief are thieves of joy, but simple childlike believing releases the joy that is resident in our spirit because the Holy Spirit lives there. As we believe that it is God's will for us to experience continual joy, we will discover a power that lifts us above our life circumstances. We will be free to leave our problems in God's hands while we enjoy His blessings.

We need to learn how to celebrate
in God's joy, to live life "to the full."

GOD'S WORD FOR YOU

I do not consider, brethren, that I have captured and made it my own [yet]; but one thing I do [it is my one aspiration]: forgetting what lies behind and straining forward to what lies ahead,

I press on toward the goal to win the [supreme and heavenly] prize to which God in Christ Jesus is calling us upward.

PHILIPPIANS 3:13-14

JOY'S ENEMY #1

Regret of the past is a primary thief of joy and peace. Many people stay trapped in the past. Whether a mistake was made twenty years ago or ten minutes ago, there is nothing you can do about it except ask God's forgiveness, receive it, forget the past, and go on. There may be some restitution you can make to the person you hurt, and by all means do so. But the bottom line is that you still must let go of the past in order to grasp the future.

Like Paul, we are all pressing toward the mark of perfection, but none of us have arrived. I believe Paul thoroughly enjoyed his life journey and ministry, and this "one aspiration" of his was part of the reason why. He had learned to forget his mistakes and refused to live in regret of the past.

Always remember that regret steals *now*! God has called us to a faith walk in the *now*. When I cling to the past, I lay aside my faith and stop believing, then lose my peace and joy.

Let this be a day of decision for you—a day when you decide to no longer operate in regret. Become a now person. Live in the present. God has a plan for you now. Trust Him today.

God gives grace and joy and peace for today, but He does not give grace today for yesterday or tomorrow. Live life one day at a time.

GOD'S WORD FOR YOU

God did not give us a spirit of timidity (of cowardice, of craven and cringing and fawning fear), but [He has given us a spirit] of power and of love and of calm and well-balanced mind and discipline and self-control.

2 TIMOTHY 1:7

Then I said to you, Dread not, neither be afraid of them. The Lord your God Who goes before you, He will fight for you just as He did for you in Egypt before your eyes.

DEUTERONOMY 1:29-30

Joy's Enemy #2

Do you look forward to every day with a spirit of joy and peace of good things to come, or do you await each morning in a state of dread? Dread, whether of going to work or facing a life-threatening illness, is a subtle form of fear that the devil uses to steal our joy and prevent us from enjoying life. It prevents us from walking in the will of God and moving forward in the plans of God to receive the blessings of God.

Dread comes after us aggressively and violently and cannot be defeated passively. Letting negative feelings and thoughts come on you will destroy all your joy and peace. We must use our faith to aggressively defeat it. We must believe that Jesus goes before us and makes a way for us. When a project seems impossible or unpleasant, trust Him to make the way clear for you.

As Christians, we can do unpleasant things and enjoy them because the Holy Spirit is in us. We can enjoy Him in the midst of adverse and unpleasant conditions. Our joy comes from Who is *inside* us, not what is around us.

If we set our minds to it, we can enjoy everything we do in life. Where God guides, He provides.

GOD'S WORD FOR YOU

And the harvest of righteousness (of conformity to God's will in thought and deed) is [the fruit of the seed] sown in peace by those who work for and make peace [in themselves and in others, that peace which means concord, agreement, and harmony between individuals, with undisturbedness, in a peaceful mind free from fears and agitating passions and moral conflicts].

JAMES 3:18

Be well balanced (temperate, sober of mind), be vigilant and cautious at all times; for that enemy of yours, the devil, roams around like a lion roaring (in fierce hunger], seeking someone to seize upon and devour.

1 PETER 5:8

THE POWER OF JOY AND PEACE

If you have a problem and the devil cannot drive you to be upset about it, he has no power over you. Your power is in maintaining a calm, peaceful, trusting attitude. The devil's power is in causing you to be upset and fearful, thus depleting your strength.

When you find yourself in a troublesome situation, let your goal be to simply stay calm. Each time you begin to feel upset or frustrated, stop and ask yourself, "What is the enemy trying to do here?"

The Holy Spirit works in an atmosphere of joy and peace. He does not work in turmoil. In a time of trial, your strength is found in taking your position in Christ and entering into God's rest. All of these biblical words—*abide, still, rest, stand,* and *in Christ*—say the same basic thing: *Do not lose your joy and peace!*

We are not overcamers, but we are always to be overcomers. You will never have overcome every obstacle, but you can have the assurance of always triumphing in Christ. If you take each problem as it comes, it will work out all right. Jesus is always with you in each situation. Just remember to trust Him for enough joy and peace for today.

❧

If the devil can control you with circumstances, he will have you under his thumb all the time. You can walk in your authority by always being in peace.

GOD'S WORD FOR YOU

You will show me the path of life; in Your presence is fullness of joy, at Your right hand there are pleasures forevermore.

PSALM 16:11

FULLNESS OF JOY

There are many wonderful benefits from simply spending time with God. The presence of the Lord is always with us, but we do not always recognize it or take time to be conscious of it.

There seems to be a great lack of joy and peace in the world but also among God's people. Many people spend their lives chasing things, when nothing can keep us satisfied except God Himself.

When people are not satisfied inwardly, they usually look for some outward object to satisfy their hunger. Often they end up in a fruitless search for that which cannot fill the emptiness within. We've heard it said, many people spend their lives climbing the ladder of success, only to find when they reach the top, their ladder is leaning against the wrong building.

When we keep our priorities straight, we discover that everything we really need in life is found in the Lord. Seek to dwell in His presence. In Him is the path of life, the fullness of joy, and pleasures forevermore.

The reason we can laugh and enjoy life
in spite of our current circumstances
is because Jesus is our joy.

GOD'S WORD FOR YOU

*[After all] the kingdom of God is not a matter of
[getting the] food and drink [one likes], but instead it is
righteousness (that state which makes a person acceptable
to God) and [heart] peace and joy in the Holy Spirit.*

ROMANS 14:17

KINGDOM LIVING

God's Kingdom is not made up of worldly possessions but consists of something far greater and more beneficial. God does bless us with material possessions, but the Kingdom is much more than that: It is righteousness, peace, and joy in the Holy Spirit.

Righteousness is not the result of what we do, but rather what Jesus has done for us (1 Corinthians 1:30). When we accept this truth by faith and receive it personally, a great burden is lifted from us.

Peace is so wonderful—it is definitely Kingdom living. We are to pursue peace, crave it, and go after it (Psalm 34:14; 1 Peter 3:11). Jesus is our peace (Ephesians 2:14). God's will for you and me is peace beyond understanding (Philippians 4:7).

Joy can be anything from calm delight to extreme hilarity. Joy improves our countenance, our health, and the quality of our lives. It strengthens our witness to others and makes some of the less desirable circumstances of our life more bearable.

It is clear in the Word of God: Seek God and His Kingdom, and He will take care of everything else (Matthew 6:33).

God will bring to pass what you are believing for according to His will no matter how long it takes. This is one of the things that will keep you flowing with joy in His Kingdom.

GOD'S WORD FOR YOU

Be careful for nothing; but in every thing by prayer and supplication with thanksgiving let your requests be made known unto God.

And the peace of God, which passeth all understanding, shall keep your hearts and minds through Christ Jesus.

PHILIPPIANS 4:6-7 KJV

Casting the whole of your care [all your anxieties, all your worries, all your concerns, once and for all] on Him, for He cares for you affectionately and cares about you watchfully.

1 PETER 5:7

PRAYER AND PEACE

The peace that passes understanding is a great thing to experience. When, according to all the circumstances, you should be upset, in a panic, in turmoil, and worried yet you have peace, that is unexplainable. The world is starving for this kind of peace. You cannot buy it; it is not for sale. It is a free gift from Jesus, and it leads to joy unspeakable and full of glory.

The prayer of commitment is a powerful prayer that moves your burden from you onto Jesus. To *cast* means to pitch or throw vehemently. The sooner you do this the better. You do it through prayer. Commit your problems to His loving care. Do this as soon as the Holy Spirit makes you aware that you have lost your peace and joy. The longer you wait to resist, the stronger the devil's hold on you will become. Then it is harder to break free.

Jesus wants us to know that we are right with God because of what He has already done for us. He wants us to have incredible peace and joy in the midst of tribulation. Only He can give us that.

❧

The believer who is experiencing God's peace through his relationship with Jesus can have peace even in the midst of the storms of life.

THE SIMPLICITY OF LOVE

*What we need more than anything else
is a revelation of God's love for us
personally. This is the foundation
for the victorious Christian life.*

GOD'S WORD FOR YOU

And we know (understand, recognize, are conscious of, by observation and by experience), and believe (adhere to and put faith in and rely on) the love God cherishes for us. God is love, and he who dwells and continues in love dwells and continues in God, and God dwells and continues in him.

In this [union and communion with Him] love is brought to completion and attains perfection with us, that we may have confidence for the day of judgment [with assurance and boldness to face Him], because as He is, so are we in this world.

There is no fear in love [dread does not exist], but full-grown (complete, perfect) love turns fear out of doors and expels every trace of terror! For fear brings with it the thought of punishment, and [so] he who is afraid has not reached the full maturity of love [is not yet grown into love's complete perfection].

We love Him, because He first loved us.

1 JOHN 4:16-19

four

THE SIMPLICITY OF LOVE

*L*oving and being loved are what make life worth living. To love is the way God created us, the energy of life. It gives life purpose and meaning. Love is the greatest thing in the world.

It is also the most fiercely attacked area in our lives. The devil's goal is to separate us from God's love, and he will use anything he can to complicate our understanding of God's love or make it confusing. His primary means of deception is to get us to believe that God's love for us depends on our worthiness.

Here's how it worked in my life. Whenever I failed, I would stop allowing myself to receive God's love and start punishing myself by feeling condemned and guilty. I lived this way for the first forty years of my life, faithfully carrying my heavy sack of guilt on my back everywhere I went. I made mistakes regularly, and I felt guilty about each one. Then I would try to win God's favor with good works.

The day of liberation finally came for me. God graciously revealed to me, through the Holy Spirit, His love for me personally. That single revelation changed my entire life and walk with Him.

God's love for you is perfect and unconditional.
When you fail, He keeps on loving you because
His love is not based on you but on Him.

GOD'S WORD FOR YOU

For God so greatly loved and dearly prized the world that He [even] gave up His only begotten (unique) Son, so that whoever believes in (trusts in, clings to, relies on) Him shall not perish (come to destruction, be lost) but have eternal (everlasting) life.

JOHN 3:16

And we know (understand, recognize, are conscious of, by observation and by experience) and believe (adhere to and put faith in and rely on) the love God cherishes for us. God is love, and he who dwells and continues in love dwells and continues in God, and God dwells and continues in him.

1 JOHN 4:16

GREATLY LOVED

Many of us believe that God loves the world, but we're not as certain about His love for us specifically. Some of us feel He loves us as long as we don't mess up. We concluded long ago that God can't be very impressed with us.

We have it all wrong. God loves us. God loves *you*! You are special to Him. He doesn't love you because you are a good person or do everything right. He loves you because He is love. Love is not something God does; it is Who He is.

God's love cannot be earned or deserved. It must be received by faith. His love is pure and ever flowing. He is everlasting God, and you can't wear Him out. Many of us think we have worn God out with our failures and messes, but you cannot do that. He may not always love everything you do, but He does love you. Love is His unfailing nature.

No matter how hard you seek the things of God, if you have not received the fact that God loves you, you are not going to get far.

Let God love you. Receive His love for you. Bathe in it. Meditate on it. Let it change and strengthen you. Then give it away.

If you had been the only person on the face of this earth, Jesus would have gone through all the suffering for you. His love for you is everlasting.

GOD'S WORD FOR YOU

To appoint unto them that mourn in Zion, to give unto them beauty for ashes.

ISAIAH 61:3 KJV

For I will restore health to you, and I will heal your wounds, says the Lord, because they have called you an outcast, saying, This is Zion, whom no one seeks after and for whom no one cares!

JEREMIAH 30:17

BEAUTY FOR ASHES

Everyone experiences some rejection in this life, and the memories and scars can be deep. Thousands of people have been hurt severely. They come from broken relationships or abusive backgrounds that are still producing bad fruit in their personalities.

The Lord has consistently taught me that bad fruit comes from a bad root. No matter how much we may try to get rid of the bad fruit, unless the root is dealt with, more bad fruit will crop up.

Some of us need to be transplanted into God's love. If we started in the wrong soil, He will transplant us so that we can get rooted and grounded in Jesus. He created us to be loved. He wants to love us; He wants us to love one another, and He wants us to love and accept ourselves. Without this root, there will be no joy and peace.

God wants to send the wind of the Holy Spirit into our lives (Acts 2:1-4) to blow away the ashes that are left behind from Satan's attempt to destroy us and to replace those ashes with beauty.

Know that you are valuable, unique, loved, and special. With this as your foundation and your root, you will produce good fruit.

*God desires to heal you from past hurts
caused by rejection. He wants you to know
He will never reject you because of your weaknesses.*

GOD'S WORD FOR YOU

If I [can] speak in the tongues of men and [even] of angels, but have not love (that reasoning, intentional, spiritual devotion such as is inspired by God's love for and in us), I am only a noisy gong or a clanging cymbal.

And if I have prophetic powers (the gift of interpreting the divine will and purpose), and understand all the secret truths and mysteries and possess all knowledge, and if I have [sufficient] faith so that I can remove mountains, but have not love (God's love in me) I am nothing (a useless nobody).

Even if I dole out all that I have [to the poor in providing] food, and if I surrender my body to be burned or in order that I may glory, but have not love (God's love in me), I gain nothing.

1 CORINTHIANS 13:1-3

THE GREATEST OF THESE IS LOVE

This is strong language, but hopefully it will wake us up!

There are many people who think they are really something because of what they have accomplished in life, but according to God's Word, they are nothing unless love has been a priority in their life.

Of course, the way Jesus sees how much we love Him is by how much we obey Him. He has commanded us to love one another; if we are not doing that, then we are not showing Him that we love Him.

We can sacrifice without love, we can give without proper motive, we can build ministries and forget all about love, but there is nothing greater we can take to the unchurched world than love. There is nothing more convincing than God's love reflected in our own character.

Love is the universal language; everyone understands it. Love can melt the hardest heart, it can heal the wounds of the broken heart, and it can quiet the fears of the anxious heart.

Love should be number one on our spiritual priority list. We should study love, pray about love, and develop the fruit of love by practicing loving others.

GOD'S WORD FOR YOU

In this is love: not that we loved God, but that He loved us and sent His Son to be the propitiation (the atoning sacrifice) for our sins.

Beloved, if God loves us so [very much], we also ought to love one another.

1 JOHN 4:10-11

GIVE AWAY GOD'S LOVE

Having God's love in us, we can give it away. We can choose to love others lavishly. We can love them unconditionally as He has loved us.

Everyone in the world desires to be loved, to be accepted. The love of God is the most wonderful gift we are given. It flows to us, and then it should flow through us out to others.

For much of our lives, we try to find happiness the wrong way. We attempt to find it in getting, but it is found in giving.

Love must give; it is the nature of love to do so: "For God so greatly loved and dearly prized the world that He [even] gave up His only begotten (unique) Son, so that whoever believes in (trusts in, clings to, relies on) Him shall not perish (come to destruction, be lost) but have eternal (everlasting) life" (John 3:16).

We show love to others by meeting their needs—practical needs as well as spiritual needs. Generosity is love in action.

God wants to pour out His love
into our lives so that we can pour it out
to a hurting world.

GOD'S WORD FOR YOU

Love endures long and is patient.

1 CORINTHIANS 13:4

Love Is Patient

Love is seen as we are patient with one another.

The world today is filled with impatient people. It seems that everyone is in a hurry. Stress levels are very high in the lives of most people, and the pressure they live under provokes impatience. Even Christians are as prone to impatience as everybody else.

Love is patient. It is not in a hurry. It always takes time to wait on God, to fellowship with Him.

A person whose life is marked by love is patient with people. He is even patient with himself, with his own frailties and weaknesses. He is also kind. He takes the time to listen to the elderly person who is lonely and wants to talk. He is willing to listen to the same story four or five times just to show kindness.

Patience is a wonderful virtue. It is one facet of love that must be developed by the person who is seeking to have a strong love walk and display the character of Jesus Christ.

Learn to respond patiently in all kinds of trials, and you will find yourself living a quality of life that is not just endured but enjoyed to the full.

GOD'S WORD FOR YOU

. . . it is not touchy or fretful or resentful; it takes no account of the evil done to it [it pays no attention to a suffered wrong].

1 CORINTHIANS 13:5

. . . forgiving one another [readily and freely], as God in Christ forgave you.

EPHESIANS 4:32

LOVE DOES NOT HOLD GRUDGES

Love forgives; it does not hold a grudge. It is not touchy, easily offended, nor is it fretful or resentful. Some people get their feelings hurt about everything. It is very difficult to be in a relationship with people like this.

We have many opportunities every day to get offended; each time we must make a choice. If we choose to live by our feelings, we will never flow in this all-important facet of love.

"Drop it, leave it and let it go," is what the Bible says we are to do with offenses (Mark 11:25). It is important to forgive quickly. The quicker we do it, the easier it becomes. A weed that has deep roots is harder to pull out than one that has just sprung up.

God is love, and He forgives and forgets: "For I will forgive their iniquity, and their sin I will remember no more" (Jeremiah 31:34). And He is glad to do so. If we want to be like Him, then we must develop the same habit.

If we are to walk the narrow path,
Jesus says that we will have to learn
to be quick to forgive.

GOD'S WORD FOR YOU

The Spirit of the Lord God is upon me, because the Lord has anointed and qualified me to preach the Gospel of good tidings to the meek, the poor, and afflicted; He has sent me to bind up and heal the brokenhearted, to proclaim liberty to the [physical and spiritual] captives.

ISAIAH 61:1

Now the Lord is the Spirit, and where the Spirit of the Lord is, there is liberty (emancipation from bondage, freedom). [Isa. 61:1, 2.]

2 CORINTHIANS 3:17

Love Is Liberating

Love offers people both roots and wings. It provides a sense of belonging (roots) and a sense of freedom (wings). Love does not try to control or manipulate others. It does not try to reach fulfillment through the destiny of others.

Jesus said that He was sent by God to proclaim liberty. As believers, that is what we are meant to do also—to free people to fulfill God's will for their lives, not to bring them under our control.

How many parents push their children to do things they do not even want to do just to meet the frustrated desires of the parents?

That is not the way true love works. It does not try to gain personal satisfaction at the expense of others.

If you and I really love something, we must take a chance on setting it free. If it really belongs to us, it will come back to us.

A caged bird cannot fly!

Proclaim liberty. Set people free and see what they do.

God wants us to release the people in our life to be all they can be for His glory, not our own.

GOD'S WORD FOR YOU

Render to all men their dues. [Pay] taxes to whom taxes are due, revenue to whom revenue is due, respect to whom respect is due, and honor to whom honor is due.

ROMANS 13:7

Love Shows Respect

Love respects the differences in other people. A selfish person expects everyone to be just the way he is and to like whatever he likes.

Respecting individual rights is very important. If God had wanted us to all be alike, He would not have given each of us a different set of fingerprints. I think that one fact alone proves that we are created equal, but different.

We all have different gifts and talents, different likes and dislikes, different goals in life, different motivations, and the list goes on and on.

Love shows respect; the person who loves has learned to give freedom to those he loves. Freedom is one of the greatest gifts we can give. It was what Jesus came to give us, and we must also give it to others.

All of God's creation has great worth and should be treated as such. Since people are the height of His creation, they should be treated with great respect and considered very valuable.

Unconditional love unselfishly loves selfish people, generously gives to stingy people, and continually blesses unappreciative people.

GOD'S WORD FOR YOU

. . . love never is envious nor boils over with jealousy.

1 CORINTHIANS 13:4

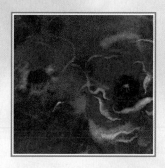

*L*OVE IS NOT
ENVIOUS OR JEALOUS

According to Proverbs 14:30, ". . . envy, jealousy, and wrath are like rottenness of the bones."

In the Word of God, we are commanded not to covet anything that belongs to another person (Exodus 20:17). We are not to be envious or jealous because these sins poison our own life and hinder loving relationships with others.

I have discovered the best way to get over envy or jealously is to admit it. When you begin to feel jealous or envious, be honest with God and ask Him to help you live free from it.

I must admit, there are times when I hear about a blessing that someone has received, and I start to think, *When is that going to happen to me?* When that thought enters my mind, I immediately open my mouth and say, "I am happy for him. If God can do it for him, He can do it for me too."

We should bless others and not be afraid they will get ahead of us. We must not envy anyone else's appearance, possessions, education, social standing, marital status, gifts and talents, job, or anything else because it will only hinder our own blessing.

We all have gifts that God has given us;
they don't come from any other source.

THE
SIMPLICITY OF
FORGIVENESS

*Forgiveness is a gift given to those who
do not and will never deserve it. Being
forgiven is as simple as freely receiving a
gift and is never more complicated than that.*

GOD'S WORD FOR YOU

In Him we have redemption (deliverance and salvation) through His blood, the remission (forgiveness) of our offenses (shortcomings and trespasses), in accordance with the riches and the generosity of His gracious favor.

EPHESIANS 1:7

If we [freely] admit that we have sinned and confess our sins, He is faithful and just (true to His own nature and promises) and will forgive our sins [dismiss our lawlessness] and [continuously] cleanse us from all unrighteousness [everything not in conformity to His will in purpose, thought, and action].

1 JOHN 1:9

five
THE SIMPLICITY OF FORGIVENESS

ne of the biggest obstacles that keeps us from celebrating the life that God has freely bestowed upon us is our own sin consciousness. Sin is a real problem for everyone, but it does not have to be the complicating problem we tend to make it.

That we struggle with our sins is a huge understatement. When we make a mistake, display a weakness, or fail in any way, we often doubt that God loves us, wonder if He is angry at us, try to do all kinds of good works to atone for our failure, and surrender our joy as a sacrifice for our error.

God wants to give us the gift of forgiveness. When we confess our sins to Him, He forgives us of our sins, puts them away from Him as far as the East is from the West, and remembers them no more. But for us to benefit from that forgiveness, we must receive it by faith.

When I was a new believer, each night I would beg God's forgiveness for my past sins. One evening as I knelt beside my bed, I heard Him say, "I forgave you the first time you asked, but you have not received my gift because you have not forgiven yourself."

Jesus bore your sins on the cross, along with the hatred, rejection, and condemnation you deserved. You don't have to reject or hate yourself anymore.

GOD'S WORD FOR YOU

My little children, I write you these things so that you may not violate God's law and sin. But if anyone should sin, we have an Advocate (One Who will intercede for us) with the Father—[it is] Jesus Christ [the all] righteous [upright, just, Who conforms to the Father's will in every purpose, thought, and action].

And He [that same Jesus Himself] is the propitiation (the atoning sacrifice) for our sins, and not for ours alone but also for the [sins of] the whole world.

1 JOHN 2:1-2

FREE

There was a time in my life when, if you asked me, "What was the last thing you did wrong?" I could have detailed the precise time I had done it and how long I had been paying for it. I worried about every tiny error I made and desperately tried to keep myself from sinning. It was not until I came to comprehend God's forgiveness that I was free from the self-analysis and self-preservation that complicated my life to the extreme.

If you believe that you must be perfect to be worthy of love and acceptance, then you are a candidate for a miserable life because you will never be perfect as long as you are in an earthly body.

You may have a perfect heart, in that your desire is to please God in all things, but your performance will not match your heart's desire until you get to heaven. You can improve all the time and keep pressing toward the mark of perfection, but you will always need Jesus as long as you are here on this earth. There will never come a time when you will not need His forgiveness and cleansing.

God's answer for our imperfection is forgiveness.

GOD'S WORD FOR YOU

For we have not a high priest which cannot be touched with the feeling of our infirmities; but was in all points tempted like as we are, yet without sin.

Let us therefore come boldly unto the throne of grace, that we may obtain mercy, and find grace to help in time of need.

HEBREWS 4:15-16 KJV

Jesus, Our Intercessor

Jesus *understands* our human frailty because He was tempted in every way that we are, yet without sinning. Therefore, because He is our High Priest, interceding with the Father for us, we can come boldly to God's throne to receive the grace, favor, mercy, and help that we need.

The "good news" is that God has already made provision for every human mistake, weakness, and failure. Salvation and continual forgiveness of our sins are gifts bestowed on us by God because of our acceptance of His Son Jesus Christ. He has forgiven every wrong thing you ever will do!

But Jesus does not want us to use His understanding nature as an excuse to stay in sin that is producing bondage in our lives. He convicts us of sin, but He never condemns us. He brings conviction so that we can see our errors, admit them, be truly sorry, repent, and receive the power of the Holy Spirit. We receive the power or inner strength by asking the Lord to fill us with the Holy Spirit. We can then allow Him to enable us to walk free from the habit that has been sin in our lives.

Even at our very best, we make mistakes. To live under condemnation, self-hatred, and self-rejection will not help us live a holier life.

GOD'S WORD FOR YOU

It is because of the Lord's mercy and loving-kindness that we are not consumed, because His [tender] compassions fail not. [Mal. 3:6.]

They are new every morning; great and abundant is Your stability and faithfulness. [Isa. 33:2.]

LAMENTATIONS 3:22-23

New Every Morning

God's mercy is new every morning. Each day we can find a fresh place to begin.

I like the way God has divided up the days and nights. It seems to me that no matter how difficult or challenging a specific day may be, the breaking of dawn brings new hope. God wants us to regularly put the past behind and find a place of "new beginnings."

Perhaps you have been trapped in some sin, and although you have repented, you still feel guilty. You may be assured that sincere repentance brings a fresh, new start because of forgiveness.

Only when you understand the great mercy of God and begin receiving it are you more inclined to give mercy to others. You may be hurting from an emotional wound. The way to put the past behind is to forgive the person who hurt you. Forgiveness is always involved in putting the past behind.

God has new plans on the horizon of your life, but you will never see them if you live in and relive the past. Thinking and talking about the past keeps you trapped in it.

Every day is a new day in God's mercies.
Don't waste today by living in yesterday's sins.

GOD'S WORD FOR YOU

Therefore, [there is] now no condemnation (no adjudging guilty of wrong) for those who are in Christ Jesus, who live [and] walk not after the dictates of the flesh, but after the dictates of the Spirit.

ROMANS 8:1

More Than Enough

Guilt and condemnation are major problems for many believers. Satan's great delight is to make us feel bad about ourselves. He never tells us how far we have come, but rather, he constantly reminds us of how far we still have to go.

When the enemy attacks, say to him, "I'm not where I need to be, but thank God I'm not where I used to be. I'm okay, and I'm on my way."

Like David, we must learn to keep ourselves encouraged in the Lord (1 Samuel 30:6). None of us has arrived at the state of perfection. We cannot perfect ourselves: Sanctification is worked out in our lives by the Holy Spirit as a process.

The Bible teaches that we can have complete forgiveness of our sins (total freedom from condemnation) through the blood of Jesus Christ. We must decide if Jesus did the complete job or if He didn't. We don't need to add our guilt to His sacrifice. He is more than enough.

Let Jesus do His job. He wants to forgive you. All you have to do is receive His forgiveness. Complete forgiveness is completely free!

Don't let the devil fill your head with thoughts of unworthiness as a sinner. Begin to see yourself as the righteousness of God in Christ Jesus.

GOD'S WORD FOR YOU

Blessed (happy, to be envied, and spiritually prosperous—with life-joy and satisfaction in God's favor and salvation, regardless of their outward conditions) are the merciful, for they shall obtain mercy!

MATTHEW 5:7

MERCY EXTENDED

Being merciful can be defined as giving good that is undeserved. Anyone can give people what they deserve. It takes someone full of Jesus to give good to people when they do *not* deserve it.

Revenge says, "You mistreated me, so I'm going to mistreat you." Mercy says, "You mistreated me, so I'm going to forgive you, restore you, and treat you as if you never hurt me." What a blessing to be able to give and receive mercy.

Mercy is an attribute of God's character that is seen in how He deals with His people. Mercy is good to us when we deserve punishment. Mercy accepts and blesses us when we deserve to be totally rejected. Mercy understands our weaknesses and infirmities and does not judge and criticize us.

Do you ever need God or man to show you mercy? Of course, we all do on a regular basis. The best way to get mercy is to be busy giving it away.

Give judgment, and you will receive judgment. Give mercy, and you will receive mercy. You reap what you sow. Be merciful! Be blessed!

Receive God's mercy and love.
You cannot give away something you don't have.

GOD'S WORD FOR YOU

[Now having received the Holy Spirit, and being led and directed by Him] if you forgive the sins of anyone, they are forgiven; if you retain the sins of anyone, they are retained.

JOHN 20:23

. . . forgiving one another [readily and freely], as God in Christ forgave you.

EPHESIANS 4:32

Keep Your Heart Free

When we hold grudges against people, are we really hurting them? Isn't it really ourselves we are hurting?

Jesus frequently spoke of the need to forgive others. If we are to walk His narrow path, we will have to learn to be quick to forgive. The quicker we forgive, the easier it is. We must do it before the problem gets rooted in our emotions. It will be much more difficult to pull out if it has long, strong roots.

Holding grudges against other people does not change them, but it does change us. It makes us sour, bitter, miserable, and difficult to be around. When we think we are holding a grudge, it is actually the grudge that is holding us. It is Satan's deceptive way of keeping us in bondage. He wants us to think we are getting even, that we are protecting ourselves from being hurt again.

None of that is true!

Ask God for grace to forgive anyone against whom you are holding a grudge. Determine from this point on to keep your heart and life free from this negative emotion.

It is impossible to have good emotional health while harboring bitterness, resentment, and unforgiveness. Unforgiveness is poison!

GOD'S WORD FOR YOU

Not that I have now attained [this ideal], or have already been made perfect, but . . . I press on toward the goal to win the [supreme and heavenly] prize to which God in Christ Jesus is calling us upward.

PHILIPPIANS 3:12, 14

Bear (endure, carry) one another's burdens and troublesome moral faults, and in this way fulfill and observe perfectly the law of Christ (the Messiah) and complete what is lacking [in your obedience to it.]

GALATIANS 6:2

TOWARD PERFECTION

"If there is one mark of imperfection, it is simply that it cannot tolerate the imperfections of others." This statement was made by Francois Fenelon in the seventeenth century. When I read that statement, it gripped my heart, and I knew it was something I needed to meditate on.

The apostle Paul stated that he pressed toward the mark of perfection. I believe all those who truly love the Lord are compelled to do that. He is perfect, and our journey into Him compels us to be like Him. We want to do things the right way—the way that brings pleasure to Him.

Perhaps a good measuring stick of our perfection is how patient and forgiving we are with the imperfections of others. When I am impatient with others because of their flaws, if I take a moment and consider my own shortcomings, I usually get patient again very quickly.

If you have an imperfection, don't be down on yourself. God will help you. If you are impatient with the imperfections of others, remember that only imperfection is intolerant of imperfection.

We need to bear one another's weaknesses, realize we all have plenty of them, and pray for one another.

GOD'S WORD FOR YOU

Confess to one another therefore your faults (your slips, your false steps, your offenses, your sins] and pray [also] for one another, that you may be healed and restored [to a spiritual tone of mind and heart]. The earnest (heartfelt, continued) prayer of a righteous man makes tremendous power available [dynamic in its working].

JAMES 5:16

CONFESSION

The passage on confession of sin in James can refer to any kind of sickness—physical, mental, spiritual, and emotional. But does he mean that every time we sin we need to confess it to another person? *No!* With Jesus as our High Priest, we do not need to go to people to receive forgiveness from God.

I believe the time to apply this passage is when you are being tormented by your past sins. Being poisoned inwardly keeps you from getting well and free in that area—physically, mentally, spiritually, or emotionally.

Once exposed to the light, sins hidden in darkness lose their power. People hide sins because of fear as well as pride, and the result is a desperate need that cries out to be released.

The practice of confessing our faults to one another and receiving prayer is a powerful tool to help break bondages. When you find a sin that maintains power over your life, you should prayerfully consider this practice. Seek out a godly person, a Spirit-led confidante, with whom you can share your soul.

It is impossible to allow poison to remain in your soul and get better at the same time!

THE
SIMPLICITY
OF PRAYER

*Pray for what God puts on your
heart, not for what everyone else
wants to put there.*

GOD'S WORD FOR YOU

But you, beloved, build yourselves up [founded] on your most holy faith [make progress, rise like an edifice higher and higher], praying in the Holy Spirit.

JUDE 20

Pray at all times (on every occasion, in every season) in the Spirit, with all [manner of] prayer and entreaty.

EPHESIANS 6:18

six

THE SIMPLICITY OF PRAYER

f you lack real joy in your prayer life, you may discover that you've allowed complexities to smother your approach. I know I did.

My first mistake was in listening to too much of what everyone else said I should be praying about. People told me I should pray about government issues, abortion, Aids, and the homeless. Others gave me a list of missionaries and their specific concerns. Some said I should do spiritual warfare. I was told how long to pray, where to pray, and that the early morning was best.

I converted these instructions into laws I had to do. It was so draining that I finally cried out to God and asked Him to teach me to pray, which is where I should have started in the first place.

He showed me that I would never enjoy prayer if I did not allow Him to lead me. The key was to pray when He was prompting and leading, for the length of time His anointing was present to do so. It was as simple as that.

The secret to a healthy prayer life
lies with approaching God simply
and gently as a child beloved by the Father.

GOD'S WORD FOR YOU

Is anyone among you afflicted (ill-treated, suffering evil)? He should pray. Is anyone glad at heart? He should sing praise [to God].

Is anyone among you sick? He should call in the church elders (the spiritual guides). And they should pray over him, anointing him with oil in the Lord's name.

And the prayer [that is] of faith will save him who is sick, and the Lord will restore him; and if he has committed sins, he will be forgiven.

JAMES 5:13-15

THE SIMPLE PRAYER OF FAITH

Sometimes when I simply present to God my need or the need of another person, it seems in my "natural man" that I should do or say more. I have found that when I pray what the Holy Spirit is giving me, without adding to it out of my own flesh, the prayer is very simple and not exceedingly long. It requires real discipline on my part to go as far as the Holy Spirit is going and no further.

My mind tells me, "Well, that's not enough, nor is it eloquent enough. And you should pray louder." The flesh generally wants to go beyond what the Spirit is giving us, and that's when we are robbed of the enjoyment that each simple prayer of faith is supposed to bring. We are to say what is on our heart and believe that God has heard us, and that He will take care of it His way, in His timing.

Children are always good examples to follow when searching for simplicity. Listen to a child pray, and it will radically change your prayer life.

Keep prayer simple, and you'll enjoy it more.

GOD'S WORD FOR YOU

Then He was praying in a certain place; and when He stopped, one of His disciples said to Him, Lord, teach us to pray.

LUKE 11:1

BE HONEST WITH GOD

If we are going to spend time in prayer, we want to be certain that our time is well spent, that our prayers are effective, and that we are praying prayers God can answer. We also want to enjoy our prayer time.

A successful prayer life is not developed overnight nor can it be copied from someone else. God has a personal plan for each of us. We cannot always do what someone else is doing and expect it to work for us. Our prayer life is progressive. It progresses as we progress, so be patient!

Often our prayers are too vague, meaning they are not clearly expressed. When you pray, be clear with the Lord. Pray boldly, expectantly, specifically. Your heavenly Father loves you, so come fearlessly, confidently, and boldly to the throne of grace (Hebrews 4:16).

If you need help with your prayer life, be honest with God. Tell Him your needs. He will help you if you ask Him to do so. Begin to say, "Lord, teach me to pray."

We need more confidence in the name of Jesus and less confidence in ourselves or anyone else to solve our problems. There is power in the name of Jesus.

GOD'S WORD FOR YOU

All of you must keep awake (give strict attention, be cautious and active) and watch and pray, that you may not come into temptation. The spirit indeed is willing, but the flesh is weak.

MATTHEW 26:41

WATCH AND PRAY

Fear attacks everyone at some time. It is Satan's way of tormenting us and preventing us from going forward so we cannot enjoy the life Jesus died to give us. Fears are not realities. They are False Evidence Appearing Real. But if we accept the fears that Satan offers and give voice to them, we open the door for the enemy and close the door of God.

Satan seeks to weaken us through fear, but God strengthens us as we fellowship with Him in prayer. Faith is released through prayer, which makes tremendous power available, dynamic in its working.

The Bible teaches us to watch and pray. We must watch ourselves and be alert to the attacks the enemy launches against our minds and emotions. When these attacks are detected, we should pray *immediately*. We may think the attack will go away, but we must remember that it is when we pray that power is released against the enemy—not when we think about praying later.

Effectively shutting the door of fear by faith will produce more joy and peace for your everyday living.

Pray about everything and fear nothing.
When fear knocks at the door, let faith answer.

GOD'S WORD FOR YOU

And this is the confidence (the assurance, the privilege of boldness) which we have in Him: [we are sure] that if we ask anything (make any request) according to His will (in agreement with His own plan), He listens to and hears us.

1 JOHN 5:14

THE CONFIDENCE OF A CHILD

We are to walk in confidence in every area of our lives. Prayer is one of the ways we can show that our confidence is in God. If we pray about everything instead of worrying and trying to work it out ourselves, we say by our attitude and actions, "Lord, I trust You in this situation."

I believe many of us pray and then wonder if God heard. We wonder if we prayed properly or long enough. We wonder if we used the right phrases, enough Scripture, etc. We cannot pray properly with doubt and unbelief. We must pray with faith.

God has been encouraging me to realize that simple faith-filled prayer gets the job done. I don't have to repeat things over and over. I don't need to get fancy in my wording. I can just be me and know that He hears and understands me.

We should simply present our request and believe that God has heard us and will answer at the right time.

Have confidence in your prayers. Believe God hears and is delighted by simple, childlike prayer coming from a sincere heart.

Ask God for what you want and desire, and trust Him to bring it in His way when the time is right.

GOD'S WORD FOR YOU

Be unceasing in prayer [praying perseveringly].

1 THESSALONIANS 5:17

PRAYER IS NOT A BURDEN

If we don't understand simple, believing prayer, the instruction to pray without ceasing can come down on us like a very heavy burden. We may feel that we are doing well to pray thirty minutes a day, so how can we possibly pray without ever stopping? We need such confidence in prayer that it becomes like breathing, an effortless action that we do every moment we are alive. We don't work and struggle at breathing, and neither will we in prayer if we understand its simplicity.

To pray without ceasing does not mean that we must be offering some kind of formal prayer every moment twenty-four hours a day. It means that all throughout the day we should be in a prayerful attitude. As we encounter each situation or as things come to our mind that need attention, we should simply submit them to God in prayer.

We should remember that it is not the length or loudness or eloquence of the prayer that makes it powerful—prayer is made powerful by the sincerity of it and the faith behind it.

We can pray anywhere at anytime about anything. Our prayers can be verbal or silent, long or short, public or private—the important thing is that we pray!

GOD'S WORD FOR YOU

Also when you pray, you must not be like the hypocrites, for they love to pray standing in the synagogues and on the corners of the streets, that they may be seen by people. Truly I tell you, they have their reward in full already.

But when you pray, go into your [most] private room, and, closing the door, pray to your Father, Who is in secret; and your Father, Who sees in secret, will reward you in the open.

MATTHEW 6:5-6

SECRET PRAYER

Although some prayers are public prayers or group prayers, most of our prayer life is secret and should be kept that way. "Secret prayer" means that we don't tell everyone we know about our personal experiences in prayer and how much we pray. We pray about the concerns and people God places on our heart, and we keep our prayers between us and Him unless we have a really good reason to do otherwise. We refuse to make a display of our prayers to impress others as the hypocritical Pharisee did in Luke 18:10-14.

For prayer to be properly called "secret prayer," it must come from a humble heart as was demonstrated in the prayer of the despised tax collector. He humbled himself, bowed his head, and quietly, with humility, asked God to forgive him. In response to his sincerity, a lifetime of sin was wiped away in a moment.

God has not given us a bunch of complicated, hard-to-follow guidelines. Christianity is simple until complicated people make it complicated.

Believing prayer is not possible
if we base the value of our prayers on feelings.

GOD'S WORD FOR YOU

Keep on asking and it will be given you; keep on seeking and you will find; keep on knocking [reverently] and [the door] will be opened to you.

For everyone who keeps on asking receives; and he who keeps on seeking finds; and to him who keeps on knocking, [the door] will be opened.

MATTHEW 7:7-8

PERSISTENCE IN PRAYER

It is difficult to lay down any strict rules on how often to pray about the same concern. Some people say, "Pray repeatedly until you see the breakthrough." Others say, "If you pray more than once, you didn't believe you got it the first time."

Sometimes when we ask God the same thing over and over, it is a sign of doubt and unbelief, not of faith and persistence. It is like the dynamic that occurs when our own children make a request of us and come back an hour later and ask again.

When I ask the Lord for something in prayer, and that matter comes to my mind or heart again later, I talk to Him about it. But when I do, I refrain from asking Him the same thing. I thank Him that He is working on the situation, but I don't repray the same prayer all over again.

Jesus' admonition is persistence not repetition. We should keep pressing on and never give up—if we are sure we are pursuing the will of God. Persistent prayer builds even more faith and confidence as we pray. The stronger our confidence is, the better off we are.

Believe that God delights in your prayers and is ready to answer any request that is in accordance with His will. Come as a believer, not a beggar.

THE HARRISON HOUSE VISION

Proclaiming the truth and the power
Of the Gospel of Jesus Christ
With Excellence;

Challenging Christians to
Live victoriously,
Grow spiritually,
Know God intimately.

JOYCE MEYER

Joyce Meyer has been teaching the Word of God since 1976 and in full-time ministry since 1980. Joyce's Life In The Word radio broadcasts are heard across the country, and her television broadcasts are seen around the world. She travels extensively, sharing her life-changing messages in Life In The Word conferences and in local churches.

Joyce and her husband, Dave, are the parents of four children. They make their home in St. Louis, Missouri.

Additional copies of this book are available from your local bookstore.

If this book has changed your life, we would like to hear from you.

Please write us at:

Harrison House Publishers
P. O. Box 35035 • Tulsa, OK 74153
www.harrisonhouse.com

To contact the author, write:
Joyce Meyer Ministries
P. O. Box 655 • Fenton, Missouri 63026

or call: (636) 349-0303

Internet Address: www.joycemeyer.org

In Canada, write: Joyce Meyer Ministries Canada, Inc.
Lambeth Box 1300 • London, ON N6P 1T5

or call: (636) 349-0303

In Australia, write: Joyce Meyer Ministries-Australia
Locked Bag 77 • Mansfield Delivery Centre
Queensland 4122

or call: (07) 3349 1200

In England, write: Joyce Meyer Ministries
P. O. Box 1549 • Windsor • SL4 1GT
or call: 01753 831102

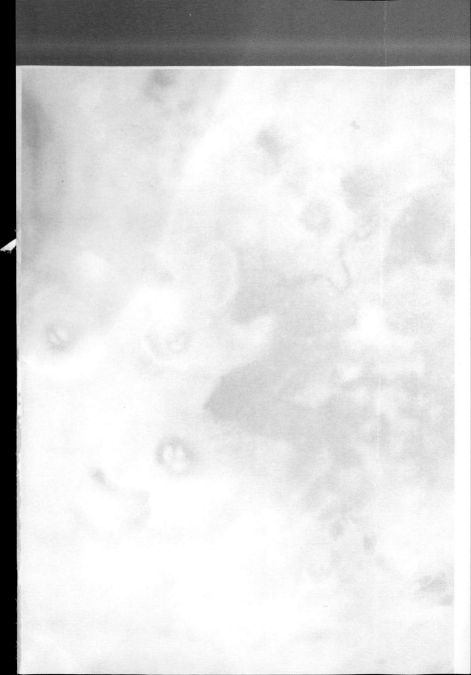

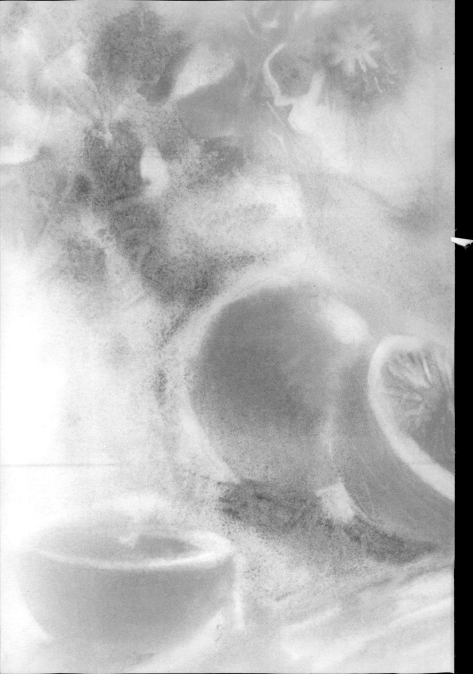